The YULE LADS
of Iceland
A Christmas Tale

First Edition Revised v2
The Yule Lads of Iceland
A Christmas Tale

Author, Cover, Designer, Typography
Adam J. Lambert-Gorwyn

Imprint
Independently Published

ISBN: 979-8-86775-248-4

Author's Note

"In Iceland's Realm,
Of Icy Dreams.
The Yule Lads Plot,
Their Playful Schemes."

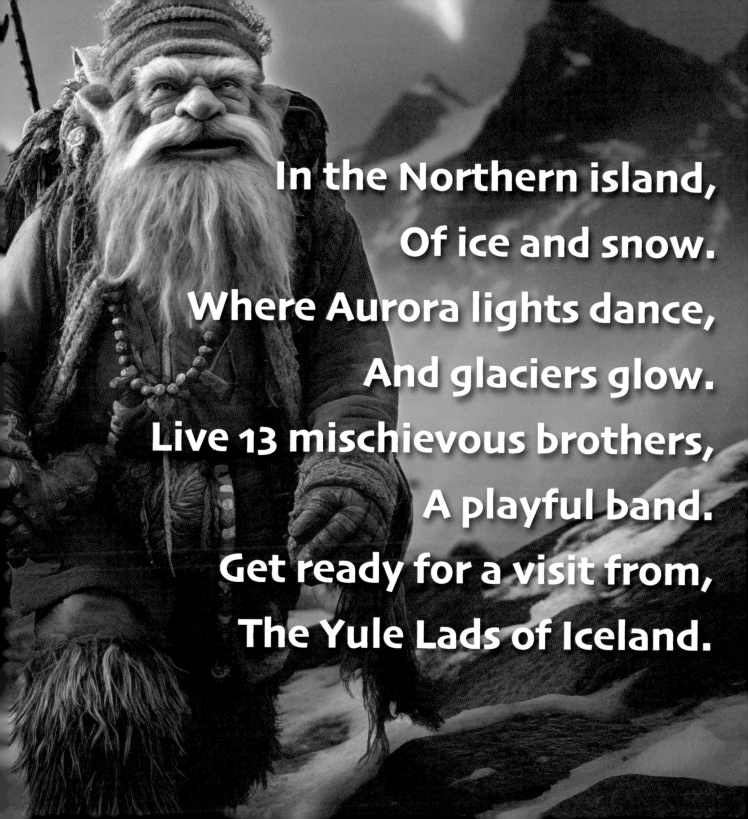

In the Northern island,
Of ice and snow.
Where Aurora lights dance,
And glaciers glow.
Live 13 mischievous brothers,
A playful band.
Get ready for a visit from,
The Yule Lads of Iceland.

12 DECEMBER

NIGHT 1
Stekkjastaur
SHEEP-COTE CLOD

Sheep-Cote Clod,
With a hobble and a hop.
He'll startle the sheep,
Until they flop.
A whirl of mischief,
He'll wobble and dance.
Leaving the sheep,
In a startled trance.

NIGHT 2
Giljaguar
GULLY GAWK

Gully Gawk,
In shadows deep.
Stealing milk,
While the cows sleep.
With a giggle and a jump,
He's quite a sight.
Under the moon's,
Soft silvery light.

14 DECEMBER

NIGHT 3
Stúfur
STUBBY

Stubby,
The tiniest of the crew.
He loves his pans,
Old or new.
Scraping the crusts,
He'll laugh with glee.
A happier lad,
You'll never see.

NIGHT 4
Þvörusleikir
SPOON LICKER

Spoon-Licker,
Tall and lean.
Licking spoons clean,
And never seen.
In the kitchen,
He'll have his fun.
Leaving none,
By the morning sun.

16 DECEMBER

NIGHT 5
Pottasleikir
POT LICKER

Pot-Licker,
He's quick on his feet.
Stealing leftovers,
Oh what a treat!
With a clang and a clatter,
Scraping with all his might.
Until every pot,
Is clean and bright.

17 DECEMBER

NIGHT 6
Askasleikir
BOWL LICKER

Bowl-Licker,
Quiet and quick.
Licking bowls,
Is his favorite trick.
Hiding under beds,
Ever so sleek.
He's the one,
The children seek.

NIGHT 7
Hurðaskellir
DOOR SLAMMER

Door-Slammer,
Loud and clear.
Slamming doors,
And spreading cheer.
Throughout the night,
His echoes ring.
Leaving behind,
A noisy ding.

NIGHT 8
Skyrgámur
SKYR GOBBLER

Skyr-Gobbler,
With a belly so round.
Eats all the Skyr,
Without a sound.
In the pantry,
He find the delight.
Eating through the cold,
Dark night.

NIGHT 9
Bjúgnakrækir
SAUSAGE SWIPER

Sausage-Swiper,
A master of stealth.
By stealing sausages,
He preserves his health.
From the rafters above,
He'll make a choice.
With every steal,
He's sure to rejoice.

21 DECEMBER

NIGHT 10
Gluggagægir
WINDOW PEEPER

Window-Peeper,
Nosy and bold.
Peering through windows,
In the cold.
Looking for toys,
And treats to take.
Leaving giggles,
In his wake.

22 DECEMBER

NIGHT 11
Gáttaþefur
DOOR SNIFFER

Door-Sniffer,
With his nose so grand.
Sniffs out bread,
Across the land.
Following sweet aromas,
He'll find his prize.
In the kitchen,
Where the loaf lies.

NIGHT 12
Ketrókur
MEAT HOOK

Meat-Hook,
With a reach so long.
Steals meat,
While singing a song.
With a swing and a swoop,
He's off in the air.
Leaving the pantries,
Completely bare.

24 DECEMBER

NIGHT 13
Kertasníkir
CANDLE STEALER

Candle -Stealer,
The last of the band.
Stealing candles,
Right out of hand.
In the dark,
He'll make his way.
Leaving shadows,
Where children play.

Remember the lads,
One and all.
As winter's grip,
Begins to fall.
Where Iceland's sagas,
Echo in the night.
The Yule Lads bring,
Christmas delight!

An Icelandic Tradition
The Story of the Yule Lads

The Yule Lads, or "Jólasveinar" in Icelandic, are a group of thirteen mischievous characters from Iceland's rich folklore, deeply ingrained in the nation's Christmas traditions. Their origins date back to the 17th century. Originally portrayed as sinister figures born to Grýla, a fearsome troll, and her husband, Leppalúði. Initially feared by children, the Yule Lads were believed to be punishers of naughty behavior.

However, their image softened significantly over the centuries. By the 19th and 20th centuries, they transformed from malevolent trolls into playful, prankster figures. This transformation was largely influenced by changing cultural attitudes and a desire to make these characters more child-friendly.

A pivotal moment in their history came with the publication of Jóhannes úr Kötlum's poem "Jólin Koma" ("Christmas is Coming") in 1932. Kötlum's work provided each Yule Lad with a distinct personality and name, shaping them into the beloved figures known in Iceland today. Each Lad, from Stekkjastaur (Sheep-Cote Clod) to Skyrgámur (Skyr-Gobbler), has a unique trait or hobby.

In modern Icelandic tradition, the Yule Lads visit children in the 13 days leading up to Christmas. Children place their shoes by the window, receiving gifts for good behavior or a potato for mischief.

Today, the Yule Lads symbolize a fusion of Iceland's pagan and Christian traditions, adding a unique charm to the country's holiday season. They continue to be a cherished part of Icelandic culture and have even garnered international interest for their unique and quirky nature.

Made in the USA
Middletown, DE
22 December 2024